Author's Guide to
SuperComputer
Translation

Greg Mills

Author's Guide to
SuperComputer Translation

Amazon Publishing House
Copyright © 2022 Greg Mills, All Rights Reserved
Independently Published in the United States of America
Author copyright inquiries: **gregmills@mac.com**
Associated Website **http://www.Lingual.Computer**

Edited by Pat Mora
Cover Art Greg Mills
All Manuscript rights reserved
ISBN 9798802068076

Forward

Founded in 2009, Amazon Publishing innovated, creating the *"Democratization of Publishing."* The revolutionary notion of on-demand digital book publishing eliminated overnight the significant investment threshold faced by self-published authors. Amazon opened the creative floodgates, empowering thousands of aspiring authors to self-publish. This created a massive glut of mostly poorly-selling books, some good, and many not, all hopelessly intermixed.

Previously, vanity publishers required a significant minimum order and still charged authors an unreasonably high price for each book. This obsolete business model forced authors to buy a minimum number of books to see them in print. The author's money was then tied up with cartons of unsold books that had to be sold to break even.

The Amazon Web Services SuperComputer allows authors the luxury of publishing their books for free. Amazon pays the author a royalty for each book they sell. This means no upfront investment and no inventory of unsold books. Amazon authors can buy inexpensive "author copies" of their books in any quantity to sell or give away. It is also helpful that manuscripts and cover art files are uploaded to Amazon's massive Web Services SuperComputer and can be updated often, at no charge. However, Amazon's publishing innovation also created intense competition. Marketing books is now far more complex than one might imagine. Selling one's books in several languages can leverage your work into additional markets.

The human manuscript translation industry is a very tough racket, best avoided at all costs. I discovered that the use of Super-Computers to translate books and avoid poor translations is now possible. Troublesome translation errors can now be virtually eliminated. It is now possible to cross-check translations, ordering a translation back to English from a second SuperComputer. We can now proof-read foreign language translations with an English language fidelity test file. That is all explained in this book. Perhaps this book is a manifesto enabling a *"Democratization of Languages"* going international.

Computer translation errors are primarily due to minor defects in the English source manuscript rather than issues in the SuperComputers' sophisticated translation software. We *optimize English manuscripts* to preempt and avoid typical computer translation mistakes. This book explains how self-published authors can re-publish their books and get into international book stores without getting a second mortgage on their homes.

Table of Contents

Introduction

Hello, I'm Greg Mills, a relatively new self-published author. I spent most of the Covid pandemic lockdown period at home in my bathrobe, nursing my coffee, hunched over a keyboard. I cranked out my first four Evangelical Christian books, now self-published by Amazon's KDP as print-on-demand paperbacks and eBooks. My translation website is: **www.Lingual.Computer**

(Note: this is not a dot com website)

Predictably, my book royalties are disappointing, actually insultingly low. I was careful to expense my allowable Schedule C self-employment tax deductions for home office, etc. Investing my savings for a while to get established was OK. However, I would hate to think that my writing was a complete financial bust.

I soon discovered an obvious but profound truth: *Publishing* a book isn't the same as *selling* a book. In this digital age of the "democratization of publishing," the competition for new authors is breathtakingly tough in just about any genre. My published English books are now available worldwide as eBooks in seventy languages, but I haven't yet tackled the audible book market.

Perhaps the "democratization of languages" is the next falling barrier standing between the thoughts of individual authors and the world's readers. That wall is being torn down by surging artificial-intelligence-powered language processing technology. This book explains how an English-only author, with an iMac, functionally obsoleted expensive human language translation and eliminated the need for human foreign language proofreading. Once these techniques are well understood, the tools needed are already available to everyone.

Various well-known book marketing programs didn't remotely pay off for me. I tried Amazon's book prioritization program shamelessly modeled after Google's Ad Word business format. Amazon offers to prioritize your "sponsored books" higher on the title search totem pole for a calculated sliding fee. I also tried using Pinterest display advertising to draw web traffic to my book website. For me, both book sale campaigns were a complete financial flop.

I read that writing more new book titles was a key to eventually building significantly more royalty income. Theoretically, the more decent books you write, the more likely one of them will be discovered by readers who will then consider buying your other books. Selling more unique book titles theoretically leads to selling more books overall.

Writing more books is an uphill struggle for most new writers. However, writing books for me is becoming more manageable. I am told my writing is also getting better. Over the last two years, I have dramatically reduced my overhead costs of writing, editing, and publishing my books. The greatest weakness of my writing project is now primarily in *selling* the books.

I am still writing new material, but I settled on an exciting concept for *publishing more titles*. Likely unique to more recent self-published authors, I figured out a more easily accessible pathway to publishing more titles than the arduous task of actually writing more new books. Theoretically, translating your published English books to be sold in international markets should create more potential royalty income.

So, I re-published my existing English books in multiple languages. Every international marketplace Amazon supports has its preferred local language(s). Various language titles can separately capture a different segment of the massive overall global book market.

One significant advantage in translating your books is that there might not be as much competition in your chosen genre in other international markets compared to Amazon.com, the largest US book-selling website. Let's consider an overview of world languages.

World Languages by the Numbers

Once an author has made the cognitive decision to translate a book into a foreign language, it is much like Imelda Marcos opening the closet doors to her obscenely extensive shoe collection. With only 365 days in a year, which shoes to wear today? To an author, the question to answer is: Which language should be translated first, and why?

Of the roughly 7,151 known languages, Google translates 133, Amazon Web Services 71, and Microsoft 110. While different translation programs support an assortment of languages, most of them are either duplicated or minor languages. Many of the lesser-known languages may not translate as well as the languages most in demand. The more a language pair is used, the better trained the SuperComputer translation becomes. The key to artificial intelligence is improving and learning as it works.

The best translation program for language fidelity is a hotly disputed metric among the larger SuperComputer companies. Various tests are run to verify translation fidelity. I have done that myself and discovered a wide dispairanency in quality between competing translation computers.

A smaller translation company out of Germany often bests the more prominent, far better-funded and much-advertised companies. Although DeepL works very smoothly, they only support twenty-eight languages. Those languages are predominantly spoken in European countries, other than the Asian languages of Chinese and Japanese. Translation services must focus on the most commonly demanded language pairs.

Statistical demand dictates which languages are best supported by all of the SuperComputer programs. It is too expensive to add minor languages for which little demand exists. English to Spanish is likely the most popular language pair with various translation companies.

FaceBook has bet the family server farm on an advanced SuperComputer with very swift artificial intelligence and massive memory capacity. It was explicitly designed to process language smoothly. It remains to be seen how well the Meta translator works and how they make their investment back.

SuperComputer translation companies generally charge an annual or monthly subscription fee, making a one-off book translation project more expensive and awkward. Those companies offering free teaser translation often limit the maximum file size. That makes translating an entire manuscript unreasonably tedious with multiple small unreadable files displayed in another language to deal with. Reassembling the bits and pieces of a fragmented manuscript will likely result in hard-to-detect cut and paste errors.

Weighing several issues is helpful as an author chooses the languages that best fit the genre and particular books they write. Market size according to raw numbers is a helpful metric, although it does not tell us the whole story. A large population that mostly can't read and can't afford books may not be a valuable market for increasing an author's royalty income.

Some authors might want to translate their books for altruistic reasons other than purely enhancing royalty income. My evangelical Christian books, for example, were not published in seventy languages to make money.

Considering first the raw numbers of the top world languages, English potentially reaches roughly 1.4 billion readers. The Chinese language groups are next. Chinese is fractured into several dialects, but Mandarin is still the most common language widely understood, reaching about 1.1 Billion. The Indian language Hindi reaches about 650 million speakers. The Spanish language potentially reaches about 550 million. French reaches 280 Million. Bengali and Arabic reach 270 million each. These raw numbers include primary and second languages that those readers understand.

Keep in mind that not everyone who *speaks* a given language can also *read* their own language, so there are obviously fewer readers of a language than speakers. However, the greater the number of those fluent in a given language, the more likely authors will gain more readers and potentially drive their international book sales.

The proportion of those affluent enough to buy books is also a factor that must be considered. The eBook publishing format serves both the least affluent and some more affluent. So, we must attempt to best serve particular language groups by providing paperbacks in the most affluent countries and eBooks everywhere. Ultimately we might try selling audible files. Each publishing format needs consideration according to the demographics of a given country or language group.

English is far and away the most helpful language for us to start with. So, authors who write natively in English will have a built-in advantage. The internet is primarily scripted in English, which has mostly driven the adoption of English as a second language. While readers will buy books written in a second language, there is a special magic in serving a person's first language preference.

According to an older World Economic study released in 2016, proficiency in English as a second language varies widely from country to country. The Dutch nation led the pack with 72% being fluent in English, Denmark with 71%, Sweden with 70%, Norway with 68%, Finland with 66%, Singapore with 63.5%, and Germany with 61.5%. This data might cause an author to assume translation into a language with a high percentage of English as second language readers are already served with the English version of their book. Why should English language authors spend money producing translated books for those who can already read them in English?

Consider now the proportion of Amazon Books sold statistically according to language. A study done in 2016 puts English books at 62%, German books at 8.3%, French books at 7.9%, then in descending order, Spanish, Russian, Italian, Chinese, Japanese, Korean and about 7% others. Since then, Amazon has launched online stores serving various language groups. There have been many more sales recently since Amazon has grown tremendously overseas in the last six years.

According to a BBC study, US book marketing numbers show Amazon sells 42% of all physical books and 89% of all eBooks. Amazon's strategic advantage in the US book market is now heavily invested in at least thirteen international stores: United Kingdom, Germany, France, Japan, Canada, Italy, Netherlands, Poland, Sweden, Brazil, Mexico, and Australia. Those numbers are likely understated since recent data indicates Amazon publishes 65% of all new books sold online in print and digital formats combined.

Most telling about Amazon's closely held strategic plan is the list of currently supported languages. Kindle eBooks are published in some languages not supported by Amazon paperbacks. This expansive list of languages might indicate future international markets of interest to authors wanting to translate English books into the most auspicious popular languages. Languages in **bold print** have at least ten million potential readers, while languages in regular type have less than ten million readers.

Amazon's paperback languages with at least ten million readers include **English, German, French, Spanish, Italian, Portuguese, Dutch, Japanese, Hebrew, Latin,** and **Swedish**.

Amazon's Kindle major languages approved for eBooks are **English, German, French, Spanish, Italian, Portuguese, Dutch, Japanese, Afrikaans, Danish and Swedish**.

Curiously, Amazon supports about twenty minor Kindle languages that don't have enough readers to pay authors royalties enough to translate English books to serve them. Amazon's paperback-approved list of languages has been expanded recently but still contains several oddly minor language choices.

Kindle minor languages include Alsatian, Basque, Norwegian, Breton, Catalan, Cornish, Corsican, Eastern Frisian, Finnish, Frisian, Galician, Icelandic, Irish, Luxembourgish, Manx, Northern Frisian, Romansh, Scots and Welch.

Amazon paperback-supported languages with fewer than ten million readers include Afrikaans, Alsatian, Basque, Norwegian, Breton, Catalan, Cornish, Corsican, Danish, Frisian, Galician, Icelandic, Irish, Luxembourgish, Manx, Provençal, Romish, Scots, Welsh and Yiddish.

I find it very perplexing that Amazon will publish Manx language paperbacks to serve less than 1800 people but completely ignore paperbacks in Bengali with 189 million readers. India is likely the hottest growing international market for books. I currently support the Indian book market by publishing eBooks in nine languages, if you also count English.

While there are about seven thousand known languages today, the top twenty-five account for half the world's population. The top eighty have at least ten million, first-language speakers, as of February 1999. Those languages with fewer than ten million readers decline in population numbers logarithmically as we go down the chart.

Although we try to present a level playing field for the world's languages, many statistically less used languages are not available yet for translation on any SuperComputer. Some unique translation issues are also notable. The definition of the term "Democratization of Languages" might be stated: the action of making language manuscript translation accessible to everyone. Languages remain a significant communication barrier standing between the thoughts of authors and the world's readers.

FaceBook has recently proposed to support *all known languages* with its new SuperComputer, which I think is very unlikely. Simply listing a language as being translatable is not the same as providing sufficient in-depth support for ideal language translation purposes. Language translation software only works in pairs. So, the memory of the SuperComputer needs enough data to develop strings between similar thoughts expressed in both languages.

Some language pairs are better supported for translation than others. My favorite language pair for translation is English into Spanish. Per the checklist, Spanish is available using every SuperComputer with advanced translation software. Spanish may have slightly more raw numbers of readers than English. Spanish speakers have a low percentage of those fluent in English as a second language. The Spanish language is well supported by Amazon for both Kindle and paperback books. Sufficiently affluent people are reading Spanish to buy our books and eBooks. This makes Spanish a perfect first language for authors to consider in translating their books.

Languages can be read right to left instead of the more common (to westerners) left to right. Arabic, Aramaic, Divehi, Fula, Hebrew, Kurdish, Neko, Persian, Rohingya, Syriac and Urdu are written right to left. That drives this dyslexic author nuts trying to post-process those laterally reversed orientation language files. It is speculated that since most humans are right-handed, writing the other way tends to smudge the writing as right-handed scribes write towards the wet ink. In antiquity, spoiling a precious animal skin manuscript was much more of a problem than modern authors wadding up a sheet of paper and nonchalantly tossing it into the trash.

Chinese Mandarin is commonly available for text translation but is a bit more challenging to work with. The raw numbers for Mandarin are substantial. While statistically fewer affluent people may be able to buy our books in China than in other countries, the raw numbers are so strong that there is still a remarkably viable market.

Amazon does not support Mandarin paperbacks, but Mandarin is in beta testing for eBooks. With nearly half the world's population speaking it, Mandarin deserves a second look despite its issues. Education and affluence are rising in China. However, the government civil authorities might suppress some subjects.

Despite the relatively low raw population numbers of those speaking Icelandic, they are statistically prolific authors. That fact alone makes me consider translating this book into an Amazon paperback for Iceland. Perhaps I will translate an Icelandic/English version of this book.

Customers willing to translate English into Mandarin will have our support. We will translate from English into any language that is readily available to us. Typically there are other personal reasons an author might pick specific languages rather than it being a purely economic purpose. I won't second guess why a particular book might shine in a specific language. Let's bait the hook and see if anyone bites.

Fishing With More Hooks

As an impressionable child, I noticed that fishermen catch more fish when they bait more hooks on their line. It seemed like adding more hooks was cheating somehow, but who was being cheated? The fish? Proof of the fisherman's multiple hook advantage was measured graphically hanging on various fish stringers. Comparing a fisherman's catch with only one hook in the water with another fisherman using multiple hooks proved the concept. The fisherman with more bait on more hooks is logically most likely to take home more fish. Buying and using more hooks is a cheap advantage.

Fishing is undoubtedly a fitting teaching metaphor for re-publishing existing English-language books into other languages. I now bluntly submit that authors don't necessarily have to *write* more books to *sell* more. Though I commonly reference the Amazon Publishing House, these principles apply to any publisher with international sales connections.

Interestingly, one quickly growing international book market is India. However, there are millions of readers of English, Hindi, Bengali, Tamil, Gujarati, Malayalam, Urdu, Telugu, and Kannada. I have recently published an eBook *in all nine of those languages.*

Serving one country with nine languages (counting English) would be financially impossible for the typical self-published author using legacy human translation services. Breaking the stranglehold of high-cost foreign language translation will bring Amazon's visionary democratization of self-publishing books into emerging markets.

Existing English books can now be cost-effectively leveraged into the various international markets. New sales opportunities are also possible by selling foreign-language titles on the American book store website Amazon.com. Many readers who speak English as a second language in the United States still crave literature in their mother tongue.

At first, the very appealing idea of translating my books appeared to be much easier said than done. My early research towards translating one of my books into Spanish was educational yet profoundly discouraging. However, as an inventor, I view dead ends differently than most people. Dead ends are, for me, only an obstacle to be overcome, not necessarily an end unto itself.

There is a famous saying: "Insanity is repeating the same mistakes and expecting different results." However, that concept flies in the face of Thomas Edison, who tested many different filaments to extend the useful life of early electric light bulbs from minutes to weeks. A reporter once asked Edison, "How did it feel to fail one thousand times?" Edison replied, "I didn't fail one thousand times! The light bulb was an invention with one thousand steps."

The first problem I encountered was the financial burden of human language translation, which was an absolute show-stopper for me. Beyond that, managing the complex translator selection process and safely paying the fees for a translator are not trivial tasks. Someone ought to write a book about it…oops, I guess I am doing just that. My ultimate conclusion is this: *Don't do it!* A much better way to translate your books is using enhanced SuperComputer language processing technology.

Authors have several significant incentives to switch from human to SuperComputer translation, starting with as much as a *twenty-to-one price advantage.* I believe the human language translation industry is doomed to become obsolete due to significant advances in SuperComputer language processing. They know industry-wide disruption is coming. SuperComputer innovation will put significant pressure on currently high-priced human manuscript translation. The popular fiction that SuperComputer translation will never be perfected is already profoundly wrong.

I initially solved the challenge of creating an improved process for SuperComputer manuscript translation for my own purposes. I was at first focused only on translating one of my Christian books into Spanish. I have since processed over eighty new titles in *seventy languages* during the last couple of years. Learning how best to do that has been challenging.

See the pull-down "languages" menu to the top right on my Christian book website at **www.Jesus2Crowns.com.** The languages named in that list each represent an eBook or paperback in that language. What I learned eventually led me to offer this same improved translation process to fellow authors as an online language translation service. I realized other authors might want to translate their books to access the international book marketplace. However, the outrageous human translation prices and complications will likely flummox them, as it did me.

This book discloses enough helpful information to enable other authors to do-it-themselves if they are so inclined. My offer to manage the SuperComputer translation process for other authors is based on my thinking that many authors would rather spend a bit of money to shorten the giant learning curve. I learned a lot about machine language translation over the past two years that would take a long time for others to figure out and fully implement on their own. It is an arduous process, *even if you know exactly what to do.*

Amazon automatically publishes new paperbacks and eBooks worldwide in its international online stores. *Each book Amazon publishes is listed according to its language.* So, language translation titles are each treated as entirely different books. That helps authors track book sales by their language. If one of your books sells well in a particular language, you might also prioritize translating your other books into that same language.

Authors select a book's language from a pull-down menu when uploading a new manuscript using your KDP (Kindle Direct Publishing) upload page. Each newly translated manuscript also gets a new, unique ISBN (International Standard Book Number) and independent placement throughout the massive Amazon publishing system.
This extensive publishing network is but a partition of the massive Amazon Web Services SuperComputer. Interestingly, that same computer also translates text files into many languages. But it is rather tricky to get it to do that. One first must subscribe to even access the portal, which is NOT user-friendly.

Amazon's KDP SuperComputer posts our new books in the most appropriate international online stores. The author sets the price in each market separately. Authors can intentionally list new books in the most prominent digital store (Amazon.com). Still, Amazon automatically places foreign books in the correct international stores, sorting each according to the book's language. For example, a book written in Spanish would upload at a minimum to the US online store, Spain, and Mexico. I focus on English as my preferred source language in this book, though the principles I discuss apply equally to other languages. English is an ideal source language for several significant reasons discussed later in detail.

Theoretically, two basic methods exist for translating books from the original English to serve additional languages. They are the storied bilingual human translation method, relying on multilingual people and the newer high-tech SuperComputer neural translation software programs.

The traditional human language translation method will soon fade away. SuperComputers with advanced artificial intelligence will shortly render human language manuscript translation services economically and functionally obsolete. When high technology can do in mere seconds what it takes humans weeks to accomplish, the economic pressure of such greater productivity will dry up human translation revenue. Voice recognition and computer-translated speech have already challenged live language translation functions. Star Trek fans will relate to the once wildly futuristic science fiction "universal translator."

The coming industrial transition to ubiquitous computer-based language translation will occur in months, or perhaps a single-digit number of years, but not decades. Humans rendering a language translation manuscript from scratch is a challenging task. It is a very time-consuming project; as we say, "time is money."

The multilingual human language translation method is as old as writing itself. The key to human translation is that some people are naturally multilingual. These talented people can hear or read something in one language and seamlessly repeat the same information in another. Human language translation is an intuitive ability based upon the intimate knowledge of multiple languages.

History's famous Rosetta Stone was discovered on July 15, 1799, in the Nile Delta region of Egypt. It featured a royal decree of

King Ptolemy V. Epiphanes. The decree was discovered in pristine condition, inscribed in three ancient languages: Ancient Hieroglyphic, ancient Demotic, and ancient Greek.

Three contemporary languages were crisply inscribed on a large flat stone. The meaning of the decree was intended to be very similar in context. Ancient Greek is well understood, so this single stone carved with examples of three contemporary written languages was a critical key to understanding two previously "dead" languages. Ancient Hieroglyphics and ancient Demotic scripts could finally be accurately deciphered for the first time. Today our digital Rosetta Stone is metaphorically housed in the memory of various high-speed SuperComputers.

This engraved stone proves that written translation between contemporary languages goes way back in human history, to at least 196 BC and likely much earlier. The scribe who wrote down the pharaoh's decree was multilingual and perhaps wrote the decree in the three languages first on papyrus paper to be skillfully chiseled in stone by Pharaoh's most skilled stone carving artists.

Many anti-machine language articles on the internet dump very cold water on the notion of computer language translation. They are written by those most interested in extending the doomed human translation industry. Note the date such critical papers were posted online. Anything published before 2018 is functionally ancient history in the case of SuperComputer language processing technology.

Also, look for conflict-of-interest disclosures, though business connections are rarely directly admitted by authors of such articles until the final pitch for their business at the very end of the piece. Their goal is panning all machine translation progress because they fear it will eat their lunch. That same fiction is also pervasive in the traditional publishing industry.

I submit that these days staring at a blank page is a foolish way to start a human manuscript translation project. This is true since a near-perfect SuperComputer paraphrased translation is readily available if you only know how to process it. Authors who customarily pay $20 to $80 a page for language translation of their English manuscripts should take notice! I now gladly offer authors improved SuperComputer language translation and cross-checking by a second SuperComputer for a flat rate of $3 per page!

In 2022, the worldwide human translation business will likely approach gross revenues of sixty billion US dollars. That number is probably very near its peak since SuperComputers will continue to improve over the next three-to-five years dramatically. The human manuscript translation model will no longer be financially viable. That is already the case for authors who know what to do.

Waxing philosophical, I might say, "He who stands too long in the middle of the road of developing technology is doomed to be run over." The time for authors to convert from human to machine translation is now. SuperComputers can do several months' worth of expert-level language translation in a few seconds, with very decent results. Even now, a higher quality artificial intelligence translation product is equal to, or perhaps better than, many mediocre human translators.

Authors will soon routinely translate their books using SuperComputer services. My flat rate of $3 per page for manuscript translation includes providing authors with an English cross-check version of the new foreign language manuscript. That way, authors can read a translation of the foreign language that has been interpreted back into English.

Google recently bragged to the press that its artificial intelligence programming equals at least average human intelligence for many tasks. They claim it has achieved self-awareness, perhaps even exceeding many people's intelligence already! Despite my typically discounting self-serving statements by Google's jaded research teams, I think they are right. See the article cited below and others.
<https://www.giantfreakinrobot.com/tech/google-artificial-intelligence-human.html>

Early adopters who welcome disruptive technology and embrace it early often cash in the most on emerging economic advantages. The economics favoring a publishing industry conversion to SuperComputer translation is indisputable. SuperComputers are closing in on having a paraphrasing accuracy equal to even the best human translators. Optimizing the source manuscript can give us the advantages of improved SuperComputer translation today.

It turns out that most translation errors begin subtly in the source manuscript text, not the SuperComputer translation software program. In other words, the adage "garbage in, garbage out" certainly applies to machine language translation.

Translation errors are dramatically reduced if the source manuscript is well optimized first. SuperComputer errors occur because something in the original manuscript's text somehow misled it. For example, computer translation software understands the context of the time frame of a passage by detecting verb forms that were used. One misleading verb tense word can result in a whole page being hysterically rendered wrong due to the computer using an incorrect time context.

Finding textual issues in a document we can't read might initially seem impossible. However, *I figured out a way to do just that.* The trick I call "cross-checking" amounts to the computer-translated text being proofed by a second computer. My proofing concept works with either human or machine-language translations. This handy computer-based proofreading process is explained in detail in later chapters. Combining optimized SuperComputer translation and cross-checking by way of a second SuperComputer provides decent manuscript translation files at a bargain price.

Problems With Human Translation

Human translation houses would glibly lead you to believe that dealing with them is an author's best possible translation experience. The truth is that getting English books well translated into the hands of those speaking other languages is currently a profoundly complicated and extremely costly endeavor. Like any business person, authors are only willing to pay for translation services that are likely to turn a profit.

I strongly suggest authors consider some significant issues before commissioning human translation services. Domestic translation houses will likely be far more professional with better customer service. However, overseas translators can generally quote a lower price. According to online complaints, what must be factored in begins with authors accepting significant financial risk and includes troublesome management issues that are likely to become a serious ongoing problem.

Oh my, talk about feeling like a babe in the woods! My initial Google search for *"Christian book translators"* garnered 135 *million hits!* I contacted several well-advertised language translation services specializing in translating "Christian" books.

I sought bids for translating my little red 115-page book with 33,350 words. I discovered many troublesome issues American authors likely face when contracting with these supposed bargain-priced internet-based human translation services. It appears to be an extensive set of challenges. Some translation houses appeared to operate in the US, but many more were overseas.

A large pool of bilingual translators advertising online is cheaper than domestic translators. I investigated that solution and rejected it for several profound reasons. At first, I didn't even consider machine translation. Reading between the lines taught me much to consider before committing to human translation. Giving up human translation left me reconsidering computer translation or forgetting the entire idea. I am so glad I didn't give up.

Some enterprising Americans have overseas relationships with bilingual locals who offer to translate English manuscripts into various foreign languages. However, I fear blindly trusting a foreign language translation service is a risky business. Authors must potentially spend thousands of dollars to determine whether their experience with a given translator will be satisfactory or an unmitigated disaster.

While searching for the means to translate my book into other languages, I learned several things that completely soured me on human translation services. The high cost is perhaps the most overwhelming issue.

Everyone in the human book translation industry will sternly warn authors that machine language translation is always inferior, and translations are *filled with hilarious, potentially embarrassing gaffes.* They advise you to avoid computer translation like the deadly Black Plague. They vehemently maintain that *only a human translator* (like they are) can help authors concisely translate their manuscript.

Perceived weaknesses in any new technology are touted defensively when any human labor-based industry is disrupted. Losing your job and seeing your work skill becoming obsolete due to emerging technology elicits strongly defensive arguments.

If you made a living translating manuscripts, would you recommend any machine translation system? These machine translation horror stories certainly give an author pause. There are even websites specializing in posting humorous stories about machine language disasters. <https://www.lingualinx.com/blog/the-funniest-examples-of-translation-gone-wrong>

Can we rely on a SuperComputer to do a credible job presenting our English manuscript in a paraphrased form in another language? The answer is no longer a cut and dried "no," since dramatic improvements in machine translation have been made recently. Even better and more accurate SuperComputer translation is coming soon.

Expecting a fantastic human language translation product for a third-world price is likely unrealistic. Generally speaking, a middleman will always find a way to get the lion's share of your funds. I suspect the better manuscript translators found online would do an honest job with at least pretty good results. However, the trick is *find-*

ing better translators. I will repeat the obvious: A bilingual person might be unable to read and write proficiently in either language. A human manuscript translation effort is quite expensive. Translating my little red "Jesus King with Two Crowns" book (115 pages) with 33,325 words calculated at 8-28 US cents per word comes in between $2668 and $9338! At those rates, human translation of all seventy target languages would set me back somewhere between $185,500 and $646,800, amounting to between $23 to $80 per page!

Financial transactions with unknown parties or third-world independent contractors could become an added source of serious problems. What could go wrong? Who can you complain to if your money is stolen? There are solutions, such as PayPal, but the more or less iron-clad safety net we experience domestically may not apply to overseas transactions.

Authors need to beware of Nigerian-bank-fraud-style activity. Google now categorically calls it "translation and interpreting scams." These charming con-men claim to be willing and able to translate English manuscripts for US authors skillfully, but they will skillfully steal you blind instead.

Author complaints confirm that the most common problem with overseas translation was that the project took much longer than initially quoted. Or even worse, the translation file was *never delivered.* Many promises were made, and much money was sent, but no translated manuscript file ever arrived.

There appears to be a near saturation level for online human translation services overseas. While this is undoubtedly true, translation prices still seemed strongly resistant to negotiations with the companies I checked out. Agreeing in advance to translate multiple books for a lower price was not agreeable to me since the quality of the service and the translation of the first book were unknown.

Then there are the twin issues of price versus quality. Would a 28-cents-per-word human translator be any better than the 8-cents-per-word service? Figuring out if the higher fee was money well spent would require a financial learning curve potentially painted with red ink.

Human manuscript translation in strong economies will always be dramatically more expensive than the cost of similar services in weaker economies. The task of human manuscript translation is very time-intensive. American translators are paid $20-$25 an hour, but the wages are just a few cents an hour in some economies.

Authors should expect human translation services to have firm financial policies requiring significant cash down payment and more substantial cash payments along the way. Don't expect a refund from overseas if the project seems to be going off the rails. Remember, agreements made over the internet between strangers halfway around the world define as an "unenforceable contract."

Delays are widespread. Most translation services quote at least a month or more from the initial down payment to the translation manuscript file delivery. The delivery date of authors' long-awaited translation commonly slips dramatically no matter when they promise it. The first author's complaint about overseas translations is the *failure to deliver the translation on time*. Projecting the date for a language translation book launch is slippery. Weak guarantees, I found, were either non-existent or vague. Some seemingly hopeful internet translator contacts suddenly went unresponsive after I pointedly inquired about the exact terms of their policies and warranties.

Communication issues are also common. The international time zones add another problem. Do you want to talk to a translator at 3 AM local time? Be aware that when doing business overseas, there are days when communication may be difficult, or even impossible. Internet and telephone communications can be very unreliable and expensive. Files are lost in transmission, and phone calls drop or won't go through.

Bias issues are potentially hard to detect in languages we can't read. All human translators have personal biases. I had one overseas translation service company owner who boasted he held a master's degree in comparative religions from a university I had never heard of. He said he would make sure my book was "correctly translated." He intended to assure me he would accurately translate my manuscripts. Instead, my inner voice raised the fear that he thought he could "correct" my erroneous fundamental evangelical doctrine to match his unknown theology.

26

I fear that a translator's educational bias or political-cultural opinions could easily seep into a translated manuscript. This "creeping-off-point" would be quite undetectable to me since I don't speak anything but English. Human language translations will always reflect, to some degree, the cultural bias of the individual. That can be charming or not.

Instead of translators substituting their ideas, how do authors find human language translation services that will precisely translate their thoughts? The bias effect could easily be unintentional but potentially just as serious. This effect goes beyond my example of literal Biblical theology, reaching cultural or radical political opinions not remotely intended to be taught by the author.

Human nature causes one's personal opinions and prejudices to color their writing. Clear, unbiased word choices are critical for correctly portraying precisely *what the author intends* or does not intend to say. This vital issue also relates to SuperComputer programming, but I think much less so than with human translators. A computer is far less likely to distort the author's intent when translating a literal thought in one language into a similar literal thought in the product language. I was infuriated that Grammarly, for a while, tried to crack the whip on using woke gender terms.

Poorly qualified bilingual translators are quite common. Beware of many individuals who only call themselves "a translator" and may not be very good at understanding your English manuscript since they can barely read English as a second language, let alone understand nuances.

Incorrect language translation can garble the intended message. A human translator's poor grammar can also be problematic in either language. A person being *bilingual in their speech does not a skilled manuscript translator make!* Poor grammar and incorrect punctuation will appear in human manuscript translations that go to print. American translators have no problem checking with the author if something is not clearly understood. Perhaps the bilingual human translator doesn't clearly understand what the author was trying to say but is too shy to admit it.

Neural Translation Magic

Some concepts and terms need to be explained going forward. Language translation from a source language file to a second language file, with the help of a computer, comes in two distinct "flavors." These general methods are the obsolete "word-for-word" statistical translation method and the newer, vastly superior neural "thought-for-thought" paraphrasing method.

"Word-for-word" statistical substitution translations are notoriously known for being a poor read and can be very hard to understand. The Greek interlinear version of the New Testament offers a classic example of a word-for-word translation from Greek to English. It is helpful for deep textual analysis and word studies but is not preferred for an easy read. No one without a Ph.D. curls up with an interlinear Greek New Testament on a rainy day and reads it for hours at a time.

Neural language machines translate or paraphrase entire thoughts rather than individual words. The practical difference between these two general language interpretation methods is enhanced user readability in the paraphrased version. The awkward word-for-word Greek interlinear New Testament compares poorly with the easy-to-read thought paraphrased "Living Bible" (Tyndale Publishing House).

Computers are great at crunching numerical data, but until recently, they were not so good at language translation. Statistical predictions linking each separate word in one language to the statistically most similar single word in the product language sometimes created hysterically incorrect meanings.

The problem is that the older word-for-word method failed to consider *the context* of the sentence being processed. SuperComputers now paraphrase entire sentences at a time. This keeps the intended context in a much tighter focus. The source file must fix anything that might derail the computer's sense of context. A long list of potentially disruptive textual issues is in the chapter on manuscript optimization.

Even Yoda, the exalted master of the Force, could be confused by the old word-for-word translation method, which also mixed the expected word order of the parts of speech in a sentence. "Understand you; what said I?"

Recent neural language translation programs simultaneously translate entire sentences, which takes much more computing horsepower. With quantum advancements in superior artificial intelligence, these high-end programs learn and improve their language translation quality with each translation they execute. They skillfully switch languages with fewer or more words than the source language file while carefully preserving the author's thoughts.

High-end neural language translation systems compete with each other. This improved translation functionality offers in many languages seamless text, speech, and voice services.

Google just announced a vaporware translation concept. High-tech eyeglasses translate the meaning of speech in another language into your language. The translation is seen in the readable text displayed on the inner surface of the lens. This requires a fast connection to the internet that isn't available everywhere yet. Typically, no product release date or projected price was predicted.

SuperComputers developing better language translation services are exploding worldwide. Amazon Web Services, IBM Watson, Microsoft, Apple, and even Facebook's server farms are developing neural language translation services to support their products.

How these competing SuperComputer programs shake out financially is yet to be seen. However, high-tech companies throwing boatloads of money at a SuperComputer language project won't necessarily compete favorably with substantial innovation made with a more modest budget.

However, the brute force behind an unlimited budget can do what was previously thought impossible. Google's recent big splash in the news claims their most advanced artificial intelligence is sentient? They say it has at least the intelligence of a child.

However, even with the promise of autonomous computers, authors simply processing original manuscript files into free language translation portals will likely have disappointing results. Optimization of the original English manuscript dramatically enhances the fidelity of all the language translations that flow from *any* SuperComputer translation program.

A critical thought, SuperComputer Neural language translation requires a near-perfect source file to render a near-perfect output file. Many, if not most, language translation errors SuperComputers make are due to subtle misleading details in the source manuscript. So, we will look at a long list of issues that can stumble even the best computers.

The context of an entire passage can be thrown off due to one word with incorrect verb tense, missing or misspelled words or even incorrect punctuation. Those dreaded mistakes can be avoided.

SuperComputer systems also have peculiar quirks to contend with. I subscribe to two very robust computer systems to access a broad range of language pairs (a source language and the translated language). I tested several other translation systems with much promise, but they failed to deliver when I tried them.

Language translation widgets are best able to process short clips. Small file size limits these free translators, best able to translate paragraphs, not book-size manuscript files. Cutting and pasting lots of short bits of a book-length manuscript, one section at a time, would be very tedious. Working with short clips is also likely to create undetected cut and paste errors in unreadable text files displayed in unfamiliar languages. That is a recipe for disastrous mistakes. So, despite the tremendous promise of these free text translation sites, there are still a few flies in the ointment. I would rather pay to be able to translate entire manuscripts intact in a single text file. The advantages are well worth the extra cost.

English manuscripts have to be well-groomed or "optimized" to support the best results for machine language translations. I think my logic is easy to appreciate as I later explain these individual issues in greater detail. I know firsthand how hard it is to catch everything correctable when editing my own English manuscripts.

Saving Money And Time

Less expensively translating my books into other languages opened up new sales opportunities in international markets. I propose to offer to other authors what I did for my books. I am rolling out an internet-based manuscript translation service for other authors. This was a logical next step for me.

I think a US-based, very competitive language translation service would sidestep the daunting issues authors face with troublesome human translation services. This is particularly true for those translators located overseas. My SuperComputer translation solution is now provided at a fraction of the typical price.

Consider my personal experience seeking to translate my 115-page American English book, "*Jesus King With Two Crowns.*" Ideally, I wanted to translate that English book into the seventy most commonly read languages on the planet, *and I did it on my own.*

I innovated by necessity, developing a method of improving the SuperComputer translation fluency of English input manuscript files. I was able to create seventy reasonably high-quality language translations. I was also able to reach breakthrough translation prices. I crushed time deadlines. I translated and published that English book into all seventy languages in about ninety days!

In the process, I got machine language translation processing down pat. I ultimately spent only about a day per language publishing each translated book. Due to the repetitive process, I worked out improved methods to process alternative language translations quickly and accurately.

The science behind this success was discovering a critical, enabling kernel of truth. Relatively minor issues in English source manuscripts "stumble" SuperComputers. Very sophisticated language software expects perfect English input documents. However, these issues are more than just providing perfect English grammar.

"Garbage in garbage out" in this context is not saying a manuscript is garbage per se, but refers to minor issues with the input

English manuscript that can result in significant problems with the computer's understanding of the manuscript. Sometimes very smart computers will do very silly things. Optimization of the English input manuscript prevents those silly errors in language translations that are output later.

I also figured out how to temporarily compress the source manuscript files, and then decompress individual product language files in post-processing to match the original manuscript's look and feel. The compression technique saves some translation fees. Amazon's SuperComputer, for example, charges for translating blank white spaces as if they were text.

I also realized temporarily removing the book's illustrations in the optimized English source file cuts down significantly on the overall file size. These graphics are all replaced in the new language manuscript files as I unpack them from SuperComputer processing in post-editing. Captions for photos will be translated as well.

Rather than paying for laborious human translation from scratch, machine translation delivers significant savings. Proofreading is generally cheaper than translation from scratch, but I innovated, doing that with computers too. Computer cross-checking language translation for fidelity is my solution to a need that arose early in my experimentation.

Being an American English-only author, how could I confirm that my freshly translated books say what I think they say? I couldn't read any of them directly, and finding a skilled proofreader for all seventy languages was neither easy nor affordable. Cross-checking is the computer equivalent to human proofreading. This is done by utilizing the power of a second SuperComputer to create a cross-check file in English solely to be compared with the original English manuscript.

Knowing the vast bulk of SuperComputer translations have proven accurate with only minor errors led me to consider publishing raw machine translation with a disclosure. However, publishing raw computer-translated books completely "blind" is worrisome. So, absent human proofreading, the process I call "cross-checking" delivers documentary confirmation that substantial translation fidelity is achieved.

Occasional spoken or written gaffs in English grammar are noticed (and forgiven) even in well-polished manuscripts and speeches. I am always amazed at mistakes in my books, even after sequential and conscientious efforts to edit them perfectly. *So what if Super-Computers make minor mistakes as well?* However there needed to be a check against seriously inappropriate content that would spoil the translation's value. We need to confirm the translation's fidelity.

Detecting translation issues in machine language files can be done by manipulating two SuperComputers rather than resorting to expensive human efforts. This solution is not dependent upon paying a bilingual person to proof new language drafts, though that can be helpful. This procedure amounts to a computerized error-checking method *with results printed out in English.*

We then visually cross-check the translation fidelity by comparing two English files. The quality of the SuperComputer language processing program can also be accurately verified. Good optimization of the source manuscript and a SuperComputer's translation file quality can be documented this way. Generally, if a source file processes well in one language, it will likely run well in other languages.

Imperfect human translators smugly criticize poor computer translations. The pot calls the kettle black! SuperComputers' artificial intelligence improves dramatically over time while human translators are not getting much wiser. I am looking forward to using SuperComputers to cross-check some human translations to *verify the fidelity of human translation.*

Cross-checking language fidelity is done by reversing a translation manuscript file through a second SuperComputer to obtain an English test file. We then compare the original English manuscript with the throwaway English cross-check file. That graphically shows us how good the fidelity of human translation is. I predict such testing will disclose that *the human translation error rate is more significant* than a raw optimized SuperComputer translation.

My computer-based proof of fidelity testing concept was used, verifying that reversing the language creates a cross-check file that works. I got the help of a skilled English/Spanish teacher, who then proofread my Spanish translation. He generally agreed with the raw original SuperComputer's English to Spanish translation. Significantly, *he also agreed with my manuscript quality testing results.*

I decided to go ahead and publish the seventy translations raw with a disclaimer in each book that the manuscript is a computer paraphrase of my original English book. It amounted to either publishing my books as basic language drafts or not publishing books in all languages. Finding and paying for seventy human proofreaders was technically preferred but was neither possible nor affordable for me.

Readers of less supported languages are thankful for books becoming available in their native language. They are asked in the disclosure notice to please advise the author of any significant textual errors they notice. If you don't gouge your readers with higher-priced books and they are advised that a SuperComputer translated their preferred language draft, readers of foreign languages tend to be forgiving and helpful.

To my knowledge, not a single SuperComputer translated book has been returned. The translation adds to the selection of books available in locally preferred languages. Substantial SuperComputer errors appear to be rare. By publishing one English book into seventy foreign languages, I saw that the neural machine language algorithms generally "crush it." That level of accuracy in processing language is improving all the time. Artificial intelligence learns and improves as it works. This means machine translation errors will become even less a problem going forward.

Some specific language pairs are particularly well vetted. Since SuperComputers learn as they translate, the more a particular language pair is used the better the translation. Vast libraries of known high-quality text files are stored for the neural language interface to learn from and refer to. This explains why more rarely used language pairs may not translate from English quite as well as more heavily used pairs. Their document reference libraries are far smaller.

For example, English to Spanish likely sees more traffic than any other language pair. I plan to retranslate my seventy manuscripts someday since significant translation improvements are being made.

Though best translated with commonly used language pairs, the neural language translation process is generally serviceable in any language pair available. Language pairs are listed at the end of this book. The convention of naming language pairs begins with the source language and then the product language. So, English-Spanish denotes an English file translated into a Spanish file.

Not all language translation computers are entirely up to speed. I have seen critical context completely flipped to an embarrassing extent. I now avoid those lesser quality SuperComputer translation programs. I use three SuperComputers and my optimized source manuscripts to get state-of-the-art translations.

Which SuperComputer(s) are best used? Many SuperComputers are advertised to translate various languages. Language translation quality varies tremendously, while advertising claims all sound similar. I tested some of the better-known language translation sites. To avoid being sued, I won't name names, but I have my personal favorites and some SuperComputers I would never use. However, advertising more languages does not imply a translation software program is better.

Manuscript language fidelity amounts to your original manuscript saying precisely the same thing in another language. This is also called "conservation of meaning" by some researchers. Functional language translation fidelity is the optimum quality we seek. This describes when the inherent thoughts in the English source manuscript are, without significant distortion, rendered into the same ideas in the selected product language.

A test page proofing a lower-quality computer system highlighted wrongly translated sections of the manuscript that completely flipped the meaning. An example might be: "Henry started the fire as I watched," which incorrectly could become "Henry watched as I started the fire." The original sentence would only be a witness statement to Henry's crime, and the second a criminal confession of the other person!

Well-written English manuscripts translate best. Crisp, short sentences, perfect English grammar, correct punctuation, and very few mysterious idioms and undefined initializations translate with fewer issues. However, there are always *some issues* to optimize. SuperComputers expect the source language file to be perfect English, anything less may render less than ideal language translation output.

I think a competitive online language translation service will be a boon to fellow self-published authors. My personal experience is related to my chosen genre of Christian books. My language translation process applies to most other types of literary subject matter, save perhaps poetry, Scripture, or other exact artistic prose.

Who knows what contextual mangling a SuperComputer might do translating famous well-written poetry? Scripture in its source language needs to be at least carefully translated and proofread by well-educated human experts. An expert should carefully proofread machine language translations of all highly critical material, for example, medical books or Scripture.

An author's worrisome reservations about the degree of translation fidelity are particularly troubling if you are a mono-linguistic American like me. I am only moderately functional, even in English, according to the goodnatured gibes of my editor! I will soon invest in another box of red ballpoint pens. She quickly wears them out on my drafts. While writing a new book and even proofing it with Grammarly, my editor's role in helping me create a solid new manuscript remains a skillful human task.

Concerns about potential translation errors are just as valid with human translators. Remember, we are not comparing supposed human perfection with something less than the technical perfection we expect from computers. Translators imply the fiction that human translations are virtually perfect compared to flakey computer translation, which is undoubtedly an exaggeration. I propose proofreading some human translations with a SuperComputer just to see what translating it back to English will show us.

Since the quality of artificial intelligence translation compares favorably with human translation, an author might consider publishing with a disclosure, "This book is created by computer language translation and has been cross-checked by a second Super-Computer." That previously unthinkable solution dramatically reduces the cost of publishing written content in other languages. We are pioneering the means to publish books in different languages primarily by using SuperComputers much more seamlessly.

I think human proofreading should only cost authors about a dollar per published page, but the price will likely run higher with some proofreaders who demand more. A dollar a page for basic proofreading seems enough to read a book and mark it up with a red pen.

Amateurs might help authors by casually proofreading books for us. Marking-up inexpensive first draft paperbacks can expedite this nicely. I hand my volunteer proofreaders a draft Amazon paperback and a red pen. I promise to collect the marked-up paperback as soon as they finish reading it. I promise I will add their corrections to my manuscript file. I will give them an updated copy of the final book when it comes out.

Although horror stories from human translators maintain that machine translation is always deeply flawed, there is little doubt in my mind that many human translators cheat. They likely begin expensive human translation projects with a cheaper machine-translated manuscript. They simply proofread it and sell it as their own work product.

In these cases, the author still pays top dollar for a far cheaper machine translation with nothing done by humans but proofreading. That is the exact translation process I offer to provide authors, but I will sell computer translation for roughly 5-10% of what human translation houses charge.

No substantial errors were found in my first Spanish language machine translation. A well-qualified bilingual proofreader found the computer's translation sound, minus a few capitalizations and punctuation differences. I was amazed and delighted to discover that my manuscript optimization and a high-quality SuperComputer worked so well.

Whenever I was unsure if the SuperComputer or my proofreader was correct, I instinctively followed the human translator's opinion by updating the Spanish manuscript. I like Grammarly, but it is too sparing with using commas as far as I am concerned. The old idea that a comma marks a place for someone reading aloud to breathe makes sense to me.

Since the initial inspiration to republish my first book in Spanish, my rough calculations indicate that as many as seven billion sets of eyes could read my *2 Crowns'* book in their preferred language! Getting my books in front of readers is the next major challenge. I must confess that I have not been able to break the book-selling distribution barrier yet. However, my material is now at least nicely readable and accessible for many people in many nations. At least two of my titles are available on Walmart's website.

Most astonishingly, I shattered the price barrier to the extent that I translated and published *all seventy alternative languages* for less than the cost of a single human translation project to publish my little English book in Spanish!

Since then, I have published my verse-by-verse Bible Study Guide for the book of Hebrews titled "*Jesus High Priest of the New Covenant*" in both English and Spanish. My most recent book, "*Jesus' Divine Powers,*" is currently available as a paperback in eight European languages.

I now feel confident translating manuscripts for others, having translated many of my books. But, I suspect not many authors will want to create seventy foreign language versions of a single book! Amazon's on-demand publishing system prints paperbacks for major European languages and posts eBooks elsewhere. I have some eBooks published on the Apple iBook store, and many international language eBooks are listed on the Kobo.com eBook store.

More people read my English "*Jesus King With Two Crowns*" book in India during one month last year than the combined sales for the rest of the world! So I re-published the original English "*2 Crowns*" book in Hindi, Bengali, Tamil, Gujarati, Malayalam, Urdu, Telugu and Kannada. Many countries' selection of Christian books is much more limited than the US market.

English language titles in any particular genre will sell much better if translated into a local language. There may be less competition in international markets for worthy books published in the local language than English on the massive Amazon.com website. A breakthrough book in one market may help sales in the other international stores.

Publishing books first in English automatically supports *at least half the world's demand for books.* English is the perfect source language to start with as we broaden our book sales opportunities in alternative markets serving the rest of the world.

English is also the world's most popular second language. So, English language books are likely to sell well even in non-English countries. According to a study, the internet, mainly displayed in English, pushes English as a second language in at least one hundred fifty countries.

Theoretically, localizing books should improve overall sales numbers. Re-publishing English manuscripts can dramatically enhance an author's marketing reach. Local book markets around the world concentrate on selected locally popular languages.

If authors only publish in English, there are a lot of missing eyes and *lost sales.* Some statistics tend to inter-mix or not discriminate the numbers for speaking and reading languages. So, the numbers vary considerably from source to source, but English and Mandarin are the first and second in any category of language popularity. From #3 down, the prioritized lists show that various languages are rated higher or lower. Many non-English eyes might want to read our books in their language if they become available.

Authors often select languages to translate, reflecting people they know. For example, Cebuano is an Austronesian language my wife spoke as a child in the central Philippines. It is also called Bisayan. Though it is way down the list of better-known languages, it is my wife's native language, so I watched for English/Bisayan to become available.

You Don't Have To Do It Yourself

Considering potential problems associated with human translation services, I offer alternative solutions to those troubling aspects. If you pay expensive human translation fees to translate your English manuscripts, fellow authors, please consider my promotional start-up prices for cheaper and potentially as good, or perhaps better, book translations.

A one-time optimization fee of $1 per published page is charged to streamline each English manuscript title to achieve better machine language translations. That is a one-time fee for each English manuscript. One optimization is good for any language translation. From that point forward you pay a $3 per page flat rate for any other language translation available.

Source file optimization allows a far smoother machine language translation into any selected language translation to follow. The fewer textual anomalies that remain in the English source file, the better the quality of the language-translation files.

We also generate and provide authors with an English translation cross-check file of each new foreign language translation. Then you can read an interpretation in English of what is being said in your target language. If you underline any troubling issues in that proof file and return it, we will fix your translation file at no charge.

1. Language fidelity is obviously an author's primary concern when translating a book. In other words, the most significant problem is that *the book must say what the author intends to say* in every language. How can language fidelity be improved?

Research indicates that SuperComputers are commonly blamed for misunderstanding the context of a passage when it was *the source manuscript that misled it.* SuperComputers may garble something not clearly defined in the source manuscript; therefore, manuscript optimization is essential. This fact is the fundamental science behind my improved translation solution. Books are more transparently translated with better fidelity when the source manuscript language is clearly defined.

2. Expensive translation fees are a very significant issue. I dramatically reduced translation prices by offering a low flat rate for machine language translation. There are two different operations involved. First, we must optimize your English manuscript and then process machine language translations from English into as many foreign languages as you wish.

3. For pre-processing optimization my start-up special flat rate is $1 per published page. For example, my English 115-page *"Jesus King with Two Crowns"* book would be optimized for $115. This produces an ideal English source file ready to submit to a SuperComputer for language translation processing.

4. For language translation and post-processing my start-up flat rate is $3 per published page. The cost is set according to the number of pages of your published book. My book, in our example, would cost $3 x 115 pages or a flat rate of $345 for each language translation. As a comparison, my language translation fee per word in US currency amounts to just over one cent, compared to eight to twenty-eight cents per word for human translation.

5. Written terms and guarantees are available in a downloadable PDF Contract file. **https://lingual.computer/services** This contract is in an editable PDF form so you can download it, fill it the blanks and email it to me to get started on a translation project.

6. Safe and secure funding can be a significant issue with overseas translation services. I require a US credit card number or PayPal information to be on file, but we only charge customers fees that have been earned according to agreed terms, and authors must approve charges first. Before sending your finished translation manuscripts via email, I bill your credit card or send you a PayPal invoice which is my last step in fulfilling a translation order.

Since I am subject to US credit card merchant terms, you have a Visa or MasterCard provider looking over my shoulder should a dispute arise. I am certainly motivated to maintain my good credit card merchant's standing. Using American credit cards alleviates the authors' number one fear of paying for something promised, but not delivered, and without having a meaningful recourse.

7. My guarantee is that should the author discover problems with individual language paraphrases, I will help fix those issues at no additional charge. Please email me or pick up the phone and call me.

8. My contact infrastructure is modern. I have a US cell phone number, and home street address for excellent communication in Kansas City, Kansas, email is **GregMills@mac.com** connecting to all my devices. Communication is supported by T-Mobile's high-speed wireless broadband. This infrastructure seamlessly allows high-speed communication and file transfer virtually 24 hours, 365 days a year.

9. The author's manuscript formatting is carefully preserved. If the original English manuscript is acceptable to your publisher, the translation file we provide will also be ready to publish. This may not be the case with many translation houses.

10. I can also inexpensively "localize" your book's cover for each language and type-set your summary on the back cover on a bid-basis. I can also create .ePub files for you so you can publish eBooks in the alternative language. The current list of languages is shown in the last chapter of this book. I reserve the right to choose the SuperComputer I think is best for your selected translation language.

11. Regarding the time factor, we hope to crush the time factor issue generally. Rather than spending weeks on one manuscript translation, with high-speed SuperComputer access, I can process as many as two short manuscripts daily! I may eventually become bogged down, but I will try to exceed expectations and deliver translations promptly. We will propose a relatively firm delivery date for each translation file ordered. I can do in hours what human translators can do in weeks. We will calendar the expected delivery date for each project as it comes in.

12. Computers are far less likely to introduce bias. We essentially take human bias out of the language-translation process. SuperComputers have less potential for bias since they are profoundly literal. They paraphrase the most logical English meaning into the most logical set of foreign words intended to conserve the author's meaning in whatever product language we process for you.

13. Nothing in the original manuscript can be left out of a language translation processed by a computer. The translated book file duplicates as much as possible the entire original file's content and formatting, visually confirmed, page by page, compared to the published English book.

14. Pre-editing focuses on optimizing content and polishing the source manuscript *before* language translation. This is to improve the quality and accuracy of the machine translation process. Any problem found and corrected in the optimized source file will automatically be correct in each language translation. Fixing issues in the source manuscript file need only be done once for all target languages.

15. Post-editing focuses on confirming the target language text file quality *after* the first SuperComputer has paraphrased it. We also strive to restore your English book's original look and feel.

16. Proofreading is critical to confirm that at least the functional fidelity of the translation has been achieved. When proofreading is done by using a computer, we call it "cross-checking". This is done automatically for each language translation we process. When we upload a finished translated manuscript for our customers, a "proof file" is provided in English. This proof file is an English translation of the new foreign language manuscript that has been rendered by a second SuperComputer. That English proof file should be read, and compared page by page, sentence by sentence, with the author's original English manuscript. The cross-check file is considered disposable and not to be published.

17. No royalties, no copyright issues, no hidden charges *ever.* This is done in Kansas, not coming from some steamy jungle overseas. My price advantage is my significantly higher productivity using sophisticated computers rather than paying slave labor wages.

Manuscript Optimization

Writing and selling books is a very stimulating challenge. There are no guarantees that translated books will sell in the international market, but let's bait all the hooks we can!

I discovered two main issues comprising source manuscript optimization for ideal computer translation purposes. They are minor mistakes in English and a long list of additional problems one might not think of. What is ok in American English books might be a problem during translation or be something that readers in other languages might not understand. We don't want to stump the computer or our foreign readers!

I discovered the efficacy of manuscript optimization when I noticed a book I was translating had a glitch in the same place in every language. I found that little error in the English source manuscript and fixed it. The next batch of translations ran without that familiar glitch. That experience led me to look more closely at other potential issues in source manuscripts that might stumble translation software.

Through practical experience, I detected a list of interesting issues while translating that book into seventy languages. Computer stumbling blocks detract from accurate machine language translation. Finding and fixing these troublemaking textual features preemptively is the crux of this process. Providing solid English grammar and removing those bumps in the road smooths the computer translation process no matter which language we translate.

I was lucky and found a patient editor who ruthlessly cuts the fat (and occasionally trims a bit of the meat) out of my draft manuscripts. She struggles to clean up my English precisely. I invested in an annual subscription to the professional version of Grammarly. That internet-connected SuperComputer language processing product corrects English grammar. That was, for me, a significant investment in my writing quality.

Grammarly fixes many potential errors *as you write,* or it can re-scan an entire manuscript. Grammarly also struggles to keep your prose in the preferred first-person perspective. It automatically fixes incorrect verb tense, finds the correct adverb, etc. While not perfect, Grammarly typically catches the most egregious English textual errors.

My grade school English teachers must be rolling over in their graves discovering that Greg Mills is writing and editing books! Grammarly allows me to produce a better first draft. The notion of pre-optimizing manuscripts for computer processing likely had its genesis in using Grammarly, a software program that resides on a SuperComputer somewhere.

Even a well-written manuscript for the American English marketplace reading smoothly to humans might still have potential processing issues when translated by a computer. These disruptive minor details commonly "stumble" ideal computer detection of context. Subtle changes may be made to your English manuscript's source file.

Textual clarification facilitates correct machine language functions. The powerful translation program must clearly understand and follow the author's intended context, or silly translation mistakes occur. Take no offense, as many books are flawless from an American English editing standpoint, but still need some smoothing out for translation purposes.

This is not *dumbing down* the content, but making minor adjustments that reduce the chance of the computer being led away from the author's intended context. Complex run-on sentences, for example, might need to be divided into two shorter sentences. This enhances both the computer's and the alternative language group's understanding.

Basic English grammar is the first sort of content clarification error we check. Contradictions in verb tense can be sorted out and resolved by English-speaking humans; but a language processing computer must decide for each passage to follow the author's context as past, present, or future. Getting the selection of the intended verb form wrong in a single word might confuse the temporal context in all future language translations until it is fixed. So, verb forms in the source manuscript are critically important clues the computer must understand correctly.

Best described as minimally modifying the book's content for improved translation purposes, the content may need to be "tuned" to aid textual processing. Language translation programs can't always correctly understand potentially misleading phrases. It still allows us room for potential clarification. The primary goal of "conservation of meaning" is carefully observed, still delivering the intended message to readers.

SuperComputer programs expect perfect English manuscript source files also reflect correct English conventions. We usually accept corrections recommended by Grammarly if they don't confuse the author's intended content. Grammarly still gets it wrong sometimes.

Undefined idioms can be a problem. We read your original English book to detect and mark undefined idioms. Idioms can be briefly explained, defined in parentheses, or slightly modified to be better understood. More clearly expressed phrases are more easily understood by other language groups unfamiliar with American English idioms.

Undefined compound words such as "bulldozer" might be briefly explained in parentheses as (a heavy road-grading machine). That prevents the indefinite dual word "bulldozer" from being mistranslated into Spanish as a sleeping bull, as a humorous example.

Common American initialisms are acceptable in your English manuscript and are not wrong. However, they may be a problem for language translation purposes. Initialisms that might stumble neural language translation computers must be spelled out. For example, KJV needs to be changed to the King James Version of the Bible. Who knows what KJV might translate to in Japanese or Swahili? I find it very frustrating reading English medical research papers that fail to define initialisms the first time they are used in an article. Making readers reread an article to figure out your secret code won't be appreciated.

Missing punctuation or wrong punctuation need to be corrected. Since neural language translation paraphrases entire sentences, we need the beginning and the end of sentences and clauses to be well marked. Sentences must start with a capital letter and end with a period, exclamation point, question mark or ellipse. This avoids sentence context being broken or confused.

Run-on sentences might need to be divided. Overly complex sentences might also be split, if smoothly possible. Creating two shorter sentences makes each shorter sentence more easily translated. Computers and alternative human language groups better understand shorter sentences. We will always strive to maintain the author's thoughts and preserve clever turns of phrases.

Accidentally doubled words, such as cut-and-paste errors like "of of" need correction. These minor gaffs might slide by in American English but still confuse SuperComputer programs that don't expect such gaffs in the English source file.

Misspelled words need to be corrected. A wholly wrong or misspelled word can quickly derail a computer's expectation of the context of a sentence. This can result in one of those hysterically badly translated sentences we seek to avoid.

Similar, but wrong, words have to be correct. For example, "through" and "though" are wildly different. Human proofreaders often miss those mistakes since they read expecting the correct word.

Terminology-related wording needs to be standardized to be consistent throughout the book. Inconsistent terminology might confuse readers from alternative cultures even if the SuperComputer gets it right.

American slang words, borrowed words from another language, or phrases with several potential meanings might confuse the computer. The SuperComputer expects to find every word in our English source file reflected in its American English vocabulary toolbox.

Identical words with multiple meanings may need to be better explained. Sometimes, a "box" is a textual square shape you use to checkmark with a pen. Sometimes a box is a cardboard carton you use to ship a gift. Sometimes you "box" someone's ears. An unclear context of the word "box" might easily create a silly mistake in translation. So we might want to change the word "box" to "carton," for example, to be more precise.

Minimize capitalizations unless needed. Never use CAP-LOCKED text in entire sentences since the computer might completely ignore all caps, thinking it is just an odd line of computer code rather than part of the manuscript content to be translated.

HTML code is likely to get messed up, but email addresses and website addresses will *usually* translate well. However, email and website addresses must be confirmed because I have seen web notations mistranslated. A website contact page www.Jesus2Crowns.com/contact was mistranslated into Spanish as Jesus2Crowns.com/contacto. That last little "o" on the translated English word "contact" would undoubtedly create internet contact errors for anyone who used the website address link that way. However, "contacto" is correct in Spanish!

Prices and currencies need to be scrutinized since they may not translate perfectly. Typically, numbers spelled out in alphabetical form, or numerals 9, 6, and 3, survive the translation process but must be verified during *post-processing*. I might flag those potential issues with red-colored type in my English source manuscript file. (Red type will always appear in the color black when published.)

The SVO rule applies. English sentences should generally comply with the convention, subject + verb + object. That word order is most easily understood. SuperComputers expect the source code file, which is known to be in English, to conform with expected word order rules. Yoda, for example, notoriously turns that convention on its head. We don't want to speak Yodaese to Super-Computers or foreign readers!

Potential issues in American English source files listed

•Misplaced modifiers
•Sentence fragments
•Incomplete comparisons or sentences
•Undefined idioms potentially not known to the subject language files
•Undefined compound or irregular words
•Undefined American English initializations: FBI, BTW, BOLO
•Mixed verb tenses, subject-verb non-agreement
•Misusing well and good, weather and whether, here and hear
•Misusing there, their, they're/ your and you're/ there, their, they're/ your and you're
•Lines of HTML code
•Weights and measures, currencies, or prices
•Confusing homophones, such as piece and peace
•Confusing similar words, using words not in their proper context
•Confusing inconsistent terminology terms
•Slang words
•Missing or incorrect punctuation
•Long run-on sentences, overly complex sentences
•Two independent clauses in one sentence without a conjunction
•Erroneously doubled words
•Misspellings
•Cap-locked sentences

Cross-checking

It is undoubtedly a great relief to hear from a human proofreader that there were no significant translation issues found. Human proofreading is unfortunately an expensive luxury when we struggle to keep the overall cost of manuscript translation affordable.

I worried it might double the retail cost of SuperComputer translation to include human proofreading even if I could even figure out a viable way to offer it. Providing human proofreading in numerous foreign languages is a highly complex endeavor and is unavoidably expensive. Despite the remarkable advances in machine language translation, finding a way of somehow double-checking the quality of the manuscript is still critical.

Humans working with me manually perform English manuscript optimization. We also post-process the new foreign language files, converting them into publishable manuscripts. But somehow, resorting to human proofreading felt backward.

However, I do want to deliver stellar turn-key service. I struggled with the issue of not being able to at least connect our author-customers with human proofreaders as part of our overall translation service. I finally gave up on both human translators *and human proofreaders*.

Early in my research, I identified a need to confirm translation fluency independently. I needed to verify the quality of thought fluency from English to product languages. The essence of this trick was devising a method to ensure the accuracy of language translations, *for languages I can't read*. I finally figured it out!

How can an English-only guy like me know how accurate a SuperComputer language translation is? Wearing my inventor's hat, I came up with a slick way to obtain a written "fluency proof file," which graphically documents the relative transparency and fidelity of a SuperComputer's translation in English so that *I can read it.* We call that method of fluency verification cross-checking.

Language fluency testing is needed to give us confidence in the translation of particular SuperComputers and language pairs. I have found that when our SuperComputer translations are proofread, most discrepancies the human proofreader finds are generally minor, such as transparent alternative synonym choices.

For example, the sentence "He mentioned me in his will" could be translated into Spanish and back to English as "He mentioned me in his last testament." The intended meaning is conserved, so the Spanish version is considered functionally transparent with the original English manuscript.

While, at first blush, the following few pages might seem a bit hard to understand, the core concept behind our cross-check procedure is that we use the first SuperComputer to translate your book. We then use a second SuperComputer to verify that the recent translation fidelity is transparently faithful to your English file. We translate the newly translated manuscript back to English to ensure it reads similarly to your original English book.

Cross-check translation verification provides a throwaway English file used only for validating translation fluency. We compare two English documents side-by-side, to see how much distortion there is between your original manuscript and the cross-check language file back to English.

Our authors can now read the English language cross-check document for themselves, which amounts to proofreading a foreign language manuscript in English.

My ultimate solution to this perplexing dilemma amounts to using a second SuperComputer to cross-check the first SuperComputer's translation product. This avoids the artificial intelligence of the first computer learning about our document before the cross-check translation is ordered. The second computer sees the translation back to English as a completely novel process. Separate SuperComputers generally don't talk to each other.

The term "language pair" is significant in neural language translation jargon. The operative notion is that machine language translation programs develop "neural pathways," metaphorically called "strings" between similar complete thoughts in various languages. These strings allow advanced language processes that link entire sentences meaning the same thing, not just using word-for-word substitutions. Translation strings between language pairs always *go both ways*. Therefore a translation system that offers English to Spanish will automatically also offer Spanish to English interpretation.

Artificial intelligence programs learn as they work. There must be "fluency" between linguistically similar phrases common to both partners of each language pair. The software strives to say precisely the same thing in the product language. These programs draw from a large memory bank of known high-quality documents to find similar sentences in both languages.

For example, when the allegorical bell is rung in an English source manuscript for the phrase "he ate his dinner," if asked to translate English to Spanish, a "neural string" rings the Spanish language bell for the phrase "se comió es cena."

Some language translation programs are far better than the rest. Several new SuperComputers are coming online soon, built with an advanced natively designed architecture optimized to tackle neural language translation tasks even better. These newer computers will likely "one-up" the existing excellent translation systems. Computers are swiftly catching up with human translators and will soon be noticeably better, breathtakingly faster, and far cheaper at performing language translation functions than humans.

Research articles consistently rate some of the better-known SuperComputer systems as much lower quality fidelity than lesser-known, but higher-quality, language translation portals. Text translation fidelity may vary between language pairs, even within one computer system. Rarely used pairs don't have as much data in the memory banks compared to more commonly used languages.

Theoretically, a shorter list of available languages might indicate more concentrated research and investment in fewer language pairs. Generally, more commonly used language pairs are better for high-quality translation. It's easy to be a jack-of-all-trades but a master of none. Some overly ambitious translation services might list many languages but actually have poor functionality between some of them.

Though I thought of using two different SuperComputers to cross-check the foreign language translations independently, I discovered later in my research that the concept was already disclosed in research literature but was not widely known. This computerized language fidelity test provides high confidence that translation has at least "functional fidelity" right out of the box.

Reversing machine language translation instructions to a second SuperComputer allows us to detect language fidelity by noting discrepancies between the original source language file and the English cross-check proof file. I will explain this concept further using practical examples.

With an ideal language translation platform, total fidelity between various languages would mean we could translate from any language to any other language with the information remaining the same.

If, for example, you had a circle of friends, the first person whispers a sentence to the person on their right, who turns and whispers the same sentence to the person to their right, and so on, all around the circle. Theoretically, the message should remain precisely the same from the first to the last person. Typically, an oft-repeated message is eventually distorted. This is true even with only a few people in the circle, all of whom speak English, let alone a series of various languages spoken back to back around the circle.

Now, consider the same scenario where bilingual friends speak all different language pairs around the circle. The original meaning would still survive intact with perfectly transparent language translation, repeating the same message around the circle by translating a different language at each point, starting and stopping with English.

Using this same principle, I sought to verify the language transparently of an English to Spanish manuscript file. We order a second SuperComputer to reprocess our fresh Spanish language file back into English. This creates a collection of three manuscripts:

1. The original English manuscript source file
2. A Spanish translation file downloaded from a first SuperComputer
3. A Spanish-back-to-English test file from a second SuperComputer

Setting the new Spanish translation file aside, we display the original English manuscript source file on the left side and the Spanish to English test file is loaded on the right side of our computer screen. We then compare line-by-line, page-by-page the original English source file with the reversed Spanish to English test file. Theoretically, those two English files should read *just about the same*, coming from a perfectly optimized manuscript and an accurate first SuperComputer translation platform.

A similarity between those two English files means the language translation process generally had "fidelity." Indeed, I typically find some word choices varied, amounting to acceptable synonyms. However, the author's intent was well preserved. The similarity of the two English files is excellent news. Reading the English cross-check file is interesting. Poorly rendered language sticks out like a sore thumb.

Theoretically, this cross-checking testing procedure doubles the number of "translation transactions" from one to two. If the inherent message is translated by two SuperComputers and is still generally similar, that indicates a very high degree of translation quality.

However, suppose there are severe discrepancies in meaning between the two English files. In that case, the source file manuscript might need to be tweaked to improve its optimization in certain places, or we might need to use a better SuperComputer. When an error in the cross-check file is noted, that issue can be detected, marked, and corrected in the optimized source file to prevent that same error from popping up in future translations.

Language translation errors could appear during the first pass of the English-to-Spanish or the second pass of Spanish-back-to-English. Although I pay for computer time for each translation when a file is processed twice, ending up with an English, cross-check file demonstrating translation fidelity is very satisfying and absolutely worth the money.

The cross-checking testing process confirms that our source file optimization is working. Our translation product's clarity also validates SuperComputer's language processing software quality. All of this can be done by an English-only guy like me! My assumption that we have achieved translation quality has been confirmed by human proofreaders familiar with both languages. While this testing was done in English and Spanish, the process will obviously also work with other language pairs.

To confirm we can detect a failure of fidelity, I tested my cross-checking verification method with a lower-rated computer translation system. I used one chapter of my known high-quality Spanish manuscript, translating back into English. I then compared my English manuscript file with the English test file.

Wow, mistakes galore. The fidelity testing method was validated, finding significant silly discrepancies on nearly every page. The test file was even rendered in poorly written English. The content also went way off my intended context. Meanings were flipped entirely in some places to become hysterically wrong. I immediately canceled my subscription to that particular SuperComputer and never looked back. So, we can theoretically also test the quality of Super-Computer translation software, not just the associated translation.

Retesting the same material using a superior computer system, I found no objectionable discrepancies between my original manuscript source file and the fresh Spanish translated back to the English test file. Except for a few minor synonym variations that still worked, the test file was rendered without violence to my book's intended teaching.

This great result was achieved without requiring human proofreading. Interestingly, verifying translation fidelity using the cross-check method might be even faster than human proofreading a foreign language, since we are quickly scanning for dissimilar wording, which stands out when there are essentially two similar documents. One need only read the cross-check file to notice the types of fidelity errors that concern us the most.

I published the Spanish version of "*Jesus King with Two Crowns*" as a "translation draft" paperback. I also gave a copy to a

Spanish pastor who teaches English as a second language. He gave me back his slightly marked-up early draft copy of my paperback three weeks later. His proofreading confirmed that my Spanish manuscript had substantial fidelity compared to the English source file, other than minor disagreements about punctuation and innocent but still logical word choices.

So, I updated my Spanish manuscript file on the Amazon book server to reflect his suggestions for the Spanish version of the book. That experience validated my confidence, encouraging me to go forward with machine language translation of my other Christian books using only the best SuperComputers.

I recently translated an English book by another author into Spanish, and we achieved a transparent translation right out of the box, meaning the process appears dependable. He has a friend who knows both languages, and she tells him the Spanish translation is solid. That was my first paying customer, and he was pleased.

I had read that better language translation programs create a nearly legal quality translation. That is certainly good enough for my books. We must remember that even when someone speaks or writes in their original language, they still make occasional errors. *So what if SuperComputers also create occasional minor gaffs?* Truth is, the original manuscripts were likely to blame, not the translation software.

I still post a disclaimer notice on the title page of the source file that is automatically translated into each subsequent product language file. This notice advises readers that the manuscript has been machine-translated and the author asks to please be notified if readers note any particularly awkward word choices.

My policy is that we will automatically make corrections to source files and language files as we discover troublesome text that needs to be improved. This is done at no charge to the author. When we send authors the language translation they ordered we include the English cross-check file for them to verify that the book's meaning is intact. Eventually, incrementally improved manuscripts should be updated with the publisher to include improvements for future editions.

There are two interrelated metrics for judging the quality of language translations, which apply to either human or computer-generated files. These considerations are similar but slightly different, teaching us about translation quality.

Translation "fidelity" relates to accurately rendering the meaning of the source text into the product language without severe distortion as to the communicative intent of the author. What is the author saying, or what are they not saying?

Translation "transparency" smoothly conforms the product file's grammar, syntax, and defined idioms to the norms of the subject language. Ideally, the product manuscript is as if it were originally written in the product language.

In a perfect world, fidelity and translation transparency would both be well served. While localized idioms and specific "play on words" might not translate quite as well, we can tweak the optimized source manuscript to at least better serve language translation purposes.

Some customers might still want to get a second opinion on the quality of the translation. I have some thoughts on human proofreading. This is where the Amazon publish-on-demand system shines again. When our most recent manuscript translation goes "live," an author can order a few "author copies" for final proofreading before considering the book published for general circulation.

Native readers hopefully can detect wrong capitalization and punctuation issues and notice significant incongruities in the text. What I worry about the most are flipped meaning issues when the language software misunderstands the author's intended context.

Most authors know someone who speaks a language they are interested in translating. I have found that bilingual friends I ask to double-check a computer-translated manuscript are commonly quite amazed that it was done so well. Generally speaking, the SuperComputer translated text is sound, but it is worrying that English-only authors like me can only confirm fidelity indirectly. However, throwing too much money at that insecurity is very wasteful.

I have found that bilingual friends who have never proofread before are still commonly willing to at least read the manuscript for me with a red pen in hand. Authors do need to remember that being bilingual and able to speak a foreign language doesn't confirm they are proficient in reading and writing either language. I fear I embarrassed a precious extended family member who spoke Spanish but apparently wasn't good at reading and writing the language. He shyly bowed out of proofing a new Spanish book for that reason.

Proofing a manuscript is far cheaper and much less time-consuming than translating an entire manuscript from scratch. Authors mainly pay for a bilingual translator's time, with a significant sum for overhead paid to the translation company. There ought to be at least a one to twenty differential in the time and money required to simply proofread an existing manuscript compared to a human's full translation from scratch.

Some higher-priced human translation services promise to automatically use a second qualified person to proofread a newly translated language file. Their fees are already so high that they certainly can afford to use human proofreading. I think cross-checking with a second computer can eliminate human proofreading as well.

Processing Workflow

I developed a sequential workflow process while translating my books. We will continue to discover refinements to this process through direct experience and experimentation.

Manuscript optimization goes beyond just repairing slightly fractured English grammar to include other subtle stumbling blocks, such as undefined metaphors that might not translate well from English to other languages and, importantly, may not even be understood in different languages and cultures.

We can translate starting with Microsoft Word or Mac Pages manuscript files. To an extent, any text to a computer is just text, data to be manipulated. A fully-formatted book manuscript file is required to begin. The source file needs to be suitable for submission to be published *precisely as it is*. I will, in return, submit your new manuscript translation file virtually ready to be re-published.

Just add a unique IBSN number and updated copyright date; after cross-checking a language translation manuscript, the file should be prepared to be published in your requested language.

English book manuscript files Amazon has approved and published are perfectly formatted. Page dimensions, font name, font size, left/right margins, gutter, header and footer settings are all inherent in those publishable manuscript files. If you send me a publishable file, it will be returned intact but in the selected alternative language.

We will not modify your original manuscript file since I need to refer back to exactly what we are starting with. We duplicate your original manuscript file, then perform optimization modifications to create an optimized English translation file with that working copy. We also need a hard copy of the English book in print for reference. With your streamlined English source file ready to translate, we also have a copy of your original correctly-formatted manuscript file. Our next step is ordering a language translation file in your selected language(s).

The optimized English manuscript file is uploaded to the most appropriate SuperComputer. The SuperComputer then duplicates the English manuscript source file, creating a second manuscript file paraphrased into the selected language and labeled appropriately. The raw translation file is then downloaded to my workstation.

The new foreign language file is opened and decompressed in a word processing program. We reset similar line breaks, white spaces and page layout as closely as possible, resembling your English book. We strive to match the appearance of your English manuscript, which is also opened side-by-side on my biggest computer screen. Page by page, we scroll through your new foreign language file and create a nearly ready-to-publish translated manuscript.

Graphics and photos are restored by copying and pasting the original file directly into the correct location for the new manuscript. I scroll through the two documents several times, confirming that the new language manuscript generally matches the original English file.

We break paragraphs and pages artistically to concisely conform the new book to look similar to your published book. We do this as much as possible considering there may be more or fewer foreign language words. We try to avoid orphaned lines. Sometimes I have to slightly squeeze a few lines closer, either vertically or horizontally, to create a pleasing and smoothy read document without wasting too many pages. The number of pages in various languages can vary. Some languages are more or less "compact," comparing one language with another. For example, once translated, my 115-page English book might be only 95 pages long in a more compact language or 125 pages in a less dense language.

Note: Optimization and language translation fees are based on the number of pages in the *original published English version of the book*. Extra pages accommodating a less compact language are not charged to our customers. A more compact language will still be billed the same amount. This allows us to use an identical fee for translating any particular book, no matter which language we translate it into.

Next, step by step how we eliminate human proofreading

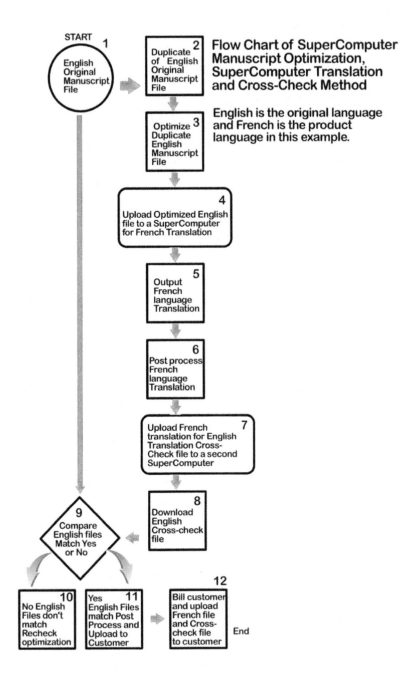

Flow Chart of SuperComputer Manuscript Optimization, SuperComputer Translation and Cross-Check Method

English is the original language and French is the product language in this example.

START 1
English Original Manuscript File

2 Duplicate of English Original Manuscript File

3 Optimize Duplicate English Manuscript File

4 Upload Optimized English file to a SuperComputer for French Translation

5 Output French language Translation

6 Post process French language Translation

7 Upload French translation for English Translation Cross-Check file to a second SuperComputer

8 Download English Cross-check file

9 Compare English files Match Yes or No

10 No English Files don't match Recheck optimization

11 Yes English Files match Post Process and Upload to Customer

12 Bill customer and upload French file and Cross-check file to customer End

1. We begin with the original English manuscript file you provided us. It should ideally match the hard copy of the published book.

2. We duplicate the original English manuscript file, saving the original file for future reference.

3. The duplicated English manuscript file becomes a source file to be optimized. We optimize your English Manuscript file. At this point, we discuss any issues we have with our authors.

4. The optimized book is compressed for processing. Your book's fully optimized source file is uploaded to the first SuperComputer, which is ordered to generate a translation file.

5. The first SuperComputer generates a language translation manuscript file which is downloaded to my workstation.

6. The new compressed language file is de-compressed. We perform post-processing procedures to create a manuscript file.

7. The post-processed foreign language manuscript file is uploaded to a second SuperComputer, ordered to create an English cross-check file.

8. The second SuperComputer reverses the translated file back into English, creating a disposable cross-check document we download.

9. The English cross-check document is compared to the original English manuscript line by line. A yes/no determination is made of acceptable translation fidelity.

10. If No, translation fidelity has not been substantially achieved. The manuscript is returned to post-processing.

11. If Yes, fidelity is satisfactory. The translation is approved; we go to step #12.

12. The approved translation manuscript and cross-check file are both uploaded to the customer, and the customer is billed.

Available Languages Pairs

Here is a list of the available language pairs as of July 2022. English can be translated into the following languages. We reserve the right to use any SuperComputer thought to be the best choice for a certain manuscript.

Most common language translation pairs requested,
English to: Spanish (European), Spanish (Mexican), French, German, Japanese, Russian, Arabic, Chinese (Simplified), Chinese (Traditional), Italian, French (Canadian), Korean, Portuguese (Portugal), Portuguese (Brazilian).

Amazon web services also support these translation languages,
English to; Afrikaans, Albanian, Amharic, Armenian, Azerbaijani, Bengali, Bosnian, Bulgarian, Catalan, Croatian, Czech, Danish, Dari, Dutch, Estonian, Finnish, French, Georgian, German, Greek, Gujarati, Haitian Creole, Hausa, Hebrew, Hindi, Hungarian, Icelandic, Indonesian, Irish, Kannada, Kazakh, Latvian, Lithuanian, Macedonian, Malay, Malayalam, Maltese, Mongolian, Marathi, Norwegian, Farsi (Persian), Pashto, Polish, Portuguese, Punjabi, Romanian, Russian, Serbian, Sinhala, Slovak, Slovenian, Somali, Spanish, Swahili, Swedish, Filipino Tagalog, Tamil, Telugu, Thai, Turkish, Ukrainian, Urdu, Uzbek, Vietnamese, and Welsh.

Google translates supported languages, English to:
Afrikaans, Albanian, Amharic, Arabic, Armenian, Azerbaijani, Basque, Belarusian, Bengali, Bosnian, Bulgarian, Catalan, Cebuano, Chichewa, Chinese (Simplified), Chinese (Traditional), Corsican, Croatian, Czech, Danish, Dutch, Esperanto, Estonian, Filipino, Finnish, French, Frisian, Galician, Georgian, German, Greek, Gujarati, Haitian Creole, Hausa, Hawaiian, Hebrew, Hindi, Hmong, Hungarian, Icelandic, Igbo, Indonesian, Irish, Italian, Japanese, Javanese, Kannada, Kazakh, Khmer, Kinyarwanda, Korean, Kurdish (Kurmanji) Kyrgyz, Lao, Latin, Latvian, Lithuanian, Luxembourgish, Macedonian, Malagasy, Malay, Malayalam, Maltese, Maori, Marathi, Mongolian, Myanmar (Burmese), Nepali, Norwegian, Odia (Oriya) Pashto, Persian, Polish, Portuguese, Punjabi, Romanian, Russian, Samoan, Scots Gaelic, Serbian, Sesotho, Shona, Sindhi, Sinhala, Slovak, Slovenian, Somali, Spanish, Sundanese, Swahili, Swedish, Tajik,

Tamil, Tatar, Telugu, Thai, Turkish, Turkmen, Ukrainian, Urdu, Uyghur, Uzbek, Vietnamese, Welsh, Xhosa, Yiddish, Yoruba, Zulu

Microsoft Azure document translation languages

English to: Afrikaans, Albanian, Amharic, Arabic, Armenian, Assamese, Azerbaijani, Bangla, Bashkir, Basque, Bosnian, Bulgarian, Cantonese, Catalan, Chinese (traditional), Chinese (simplified), Croatian, Danish, Dari, Divehi, Dutch, English, Estonian, Faroese, Fijian, Filipino, Finnish, French, French (Canada), Galician, Georgian, German, Greek, Gujarati, Haitian Creole, Hebrew, Hindi, Hmong Daw, Hungarian, Icelandic, Indonesian, Interlingua, Inuktitut, Irish, Italian, Japanese, Kannada, Kazakh, Khmer, Korean, Kurdish, Kyrgyz, Lao, Latvian, Lithuanian, Macedonian, Malagasy, Malayalam, Maltese, Maori, Marathi, Mongolian, Myanmar, Nepali, Norwegian, Odia, Pashto, Persian, Polish, Portuguese Brazilian, Portuguese, Punjabi, Queretaro Otomi, Romanian, Russian, Samoan, Serbian, Slovak, Slovenian, Somoli, Spanish, Swahili, Swedish, Tahitian, Tamil, Tatar, Telugu, Thai, Tibetan, Tigrinya, Tonga, Turkish, Turkmen, Ukrainian, Sorbian, Urdu, Usbek, Vietnamese, Welsh, Yucatec Maya, Zulu

The languages and best SuperComputers for us to use are moving targets. I will try to stay on top of that to achieve the best quality translations we can provide. An author wanting to discuss my translation services should feel free to call me. We can discuss your goals, and I can answer your questions. My contract form for services is found at my translation website: **www.Lingual.Computer**
(Note: this website address is not dot com, it is a dot computer URL)

Greg Mills
9639 Georgia Ave.
Kansas City, Kansas 66109
gregmills@mac.com
913-915-8474

Printed in Great Britain
by Amazon

44354995R00036